UNDERSTANDING AMERICAN DEMOCRACY

SEPARATION OF GOVERNMENT POWERS

by Christy Mihaly

San Diego, CA

© 2024 BrightPoint Press
an imprint of ReferencePoint Press, Inc.
Printed in the United States

For more information, contact:
BrightPoint Press
PO Box 27779
San Diego, CA 92198
www.BrightPointPress.com

ALL RIGHTS RESERVED.

No part of this work covered by the copyright hereon may be reproduced or used in any form or by any means—graphic, electronic, or mechanical, including photocopying, recording, taping, web distribution, or information storage retrieval systems—without the written permission of the publisher.

LIBRARY OF CONGRESS CATALOGING-IN-PUBLICATION DATA

Names: Mihaly, Christy, author.
Title: Separation of government powers / by Christy Mihaly.
Description: San Diego, CA: BrightPoint Press, 2024. | Series: Understanding American democracy | Includes bibliographical references and index. | Audience: Ages 13 | Audience: Grades 7-9
Identifiers: LCCN 2023012477 (print) | LCCN 2023012478 (eBook) | ISBN 9781678207007 (hardcover) | ISBN 9781678207014 (eBook)
Subjects: LCSH: United States--Politics and government--Juvenile literature. | Separation of powers--United States--Juvenile literature.
Classification: LCC JK305 .M55 2024 (print) | LCC JK305 (eBook) | DDC 320.473--dc23/eng/20230320
LC record available at https://lccn.loc.gov/2023012477
LC eBook record available at https://lccn.loc.gov/2023012478

CONTENTS

AT A GLANCE	4
INTRODUCTION ONE GOVERNMENT, THREE BRANCHES	6
CHAPTER ONE THE LEGISLATIVE BRANCH	12
CHAPTER TWO THE EXECUTIVE BRANCH	26
CHAPTER THREE THE JUDICIAL BRANCH	40
CHAPTER FOUR BALANCING THE BRANCHES	50
Glossary	58
Source Notes	59
For Further Research	60
Index	62
Image Credits	63
About the Author	64

AT A GLANCE

- The US Constitution divides the government into three branches. These are the legislative branch, executive branch, and judicial branch. Each branch has its own powers.

- The Constitution creates a system of checks and balances among the three branches. This prevents any one branch from having too much power.

- Congress is the legislative branch of government. It makes laws. Congress is responsible for the national budget. It also can impeach federal officials, approve or reject presidential appointments and treaties, and declare war.

- Members of Congress are elected by US citizens. Congress members represent the people who elect them.

- The president is the head of state and leads the executive branch. This branch applies the laws.

- The president is elected, but most of the executive branch is not. This branch has about 400 agencies and more than 4 million workers.

- The judicial branch is made up of the courts. This branch interprets the laws. There are three levels of federal courts. The Supreme Court is the highest court.

- Federal judges are not elected. They are appointed for life terms.

- The push and pull among the three branches shapes the US government and its laws.

INTRODUCTION

ONE GOVERNMENT, THREE BRANCHES

Skylar is watching TV. Suddenly, a news update flashes across the screen. The US Congress has passed a law. The law will help fight climate change.

But the news report goes on. It says that the president opposes the law. She plans to veto, or reject, the law. Meanwhile, oil companies are asking a court to stop the law.

Wait! Skylar thinks. This makes no sense. Congress makes the laws. How can the president or courts interfere?

Then Skylar remembers more about the government's powers. They are separated into three branches. Congress is the

Congress is the legislative branch of the US government. Members of Congress are responsible for making laws.

legislative branch. The president leads the executive branch. The courts form the judicial branch. The three branches are equally important. And sometimes one branch can overrule another.

Skylar turns off the TV and opens her laptop. She will write to the people who represent her in Congress. She'll urge them to override the president's veto.

THE US GOVERNMENT

The structure of the US government is described in the Constitution. This document is the highest law of the nation.

GOVERNMENT BRANCHES AND LEVELS

	Legislative Branch	Executive Branch	Judicial Branch
Federal Government	Congress (Senate and House of Representatives)	President, vice president, executive officials, executive agencies	Supreme Court, courts of appeals, district courts, other federal courts
State Government	State legislature	State governor, state officials, state agencies	State courts
Local Government	City council, town selectboard, county supervisors	Mayor, city officials, departments, agencies	City or municipal courts

The US government is divided into three branches. Each branch has different roles in federal, state, and local governments.

The Constitution creates Congress. It gives Congress the power to make laws. The Constitution also says the executive branch will carry out laws. It sets up the judicial branch too. This includes the courts, which interpret the laws. The Constitution creates a system of checks and balances too. This means no branch is more powerful than the others.

Before the United States became a country, there were thirteen colonies in North America. These colonies were ruled by England. The colonists wanted a say in how they were governed. They believed England treated them unjustly. This led to the Revolutionary War (1775–1783). The colonists fought for independence from England. The colonists won the war. They established a new country. The nation's

The Constitution begins with the words "We the People."

founders wrote the Constitution in 1787. It said that the country's people would rule themselves rather than obeying a king. It also limited the government's power. This would help protect people's rights. It is a key idea in US democracy.

1
THE LEGISLATIVE BRANCH

The Constitution includes seven sections called Articles. Article I of the Constitution gives Congress the government's legislative power. This is the lawmaking power. Only Congress can make or change the nation's laws.

TWO HOUSES OF CONGRESS

Congress is made up of two groups. These are sometimes called houses. They are known as the Senate and the House of Representatives. Each state's voters elect members of Congress to represent them.

Both houses of Congress meet in the US Capitol building in Washington, DC.

The leader of the House of Representatives is the Speaker of the House. In 2023, Republican Kevin McCarthy was elected Speaker of the House.

Each state elects two people to the Senate. Members of the Senate are called senators. A senator represents an entire state. There are one hundred senators in the Senate. They serve for six-year terms.

Every two years, there are elections for about one-third of the Senate seats.

The House of Representatives has 435 voting members. Representatives are elected every two years. Each one represents a home district. About 760,000 people live in an average district. The number of districts in a state depends on its population. The population is the number of people that live in a state. The seven states with the smallest populations each have one representative. California has the largest state population. In 2022, California elected fifty-three representatives.

CONGRESS IN ACTION

Congress's main job is making laws. The Constitution lists the types of laws that Congress can pass. For example, Congress can set up post offices. But the founders didn't know what laws would be needed in the future. So they said Congress could

NONVOTING HOUSE MEMBERS

The House includes five nonvoting **delegates**. They represent Washington, DC, and the US territories of Guam, American Samoa, the US Virgin Islands, and the Northern Mariana Islands. A resident commissioner represents Puerto Rico. These members may introduce bills and vote in **committees**. But they cannot vote on final bills.

"make all Laws which shall be necessary and proper."[1] This gives Congress a lot of power. Congress has passed many laws. Some laws involve the military and the environment. There are laws about health care, gun control, and taxes too.

HOW LAWS ARE MADE

A law starts as an idea. Sometimes the idea comes from a voter. Then a member of Congress writes the idea into a bill. A bill is a proposed law. The member introduces the bill. A senator's bill goes to the Senate. A representative's bill goes to the House.

Next, the bill is assigned to a committee. There are Senate committees and House committees. Different committees study bills on different topics. The committees hold hearings. These are meetings where people talk about proposed laws. Experts often speak at these meetings.

Committees often make changes to a bill. Then committee members vote on it. Sometimes they vote against the bill. When this happens, the bill dies in committee. If they support the bill, they vote to pass it out of committee. Then the bill is ready to be considered by Congress.

One Senate committee is the Committee on the Judiciary. It considers nominations for positions in the executive and judicial branches.

The next step is debate. First, the bill is debated by the house in which it was introduced. House and Senate leaders decide which bills their house will debate. During debates, supporters and opponents speak about the bill. They may offer changes to it. They vote on the changes. Then they vote on the bill. If the bill passes in one house, it moves to the other house. If either house votes the bill down, it fails.

Sometimes both houses pass a bill. When this happens, they usually pass slightly different versions. For the bill to become law, both houses must approve the same words. So a conference committee goes to work. Senate and House members read both versions of the bill. Then they write the final bill. Both houses vote on the final version. If it passes, the bill goes to

Once a bill passes in the House and Senate, it goes to the president for approval.

the president. If the president signs it, the bill becomes law.

A president may refuse to sign a bill. This is the veto power. But Congress can override a veto. This means Congress can pass the law even after the president has vetoed it. An override requires a two-thirds vote from each house.

CHECKS AND BALANCES

James Madison was one of the founding fathers who wrote the Constitution. He went on to become the fourth president. He warned that putting "all powers, legislative, executive, and judiciary, in the same hands" is "the very definition of **tyranny**."[2] Separating the powers prevents this from happening. Checks and balances allow each branch to limit the power of the others.

For example, Congress can impeach government officials. They can remove them from their positions. The Constitution says Congress can impeach someone for "Treason, Bribery, or other high Crimes and Misdemeanors."[3] The House brings impeachment charges. Then the Senate

OTHER POWERS OF CONGRESS

The Constitution gives Congress important powers beyond lawmaking. Congress controls the nation's money. It has the power to impose federal taxes. Congress also writes the government's budget, which determines how the government spends its money. The Constitution states that only Congress has the power to declare war.

In 2019 and 2021, the House voted to impeach President Donald Trump. He is the only US president to be impeached twice.

holds a trial. It votes on whether to remove the official from office.

The Senate can overrule the president's power in other ways too. For example, the president **nominates** people for government roles. The Senate can confirm or reject these nominations. The president can also agree to **treaties** with other nations. But treaties must be approved by two-thirds of the Senate.

2
THE EXECUTIVE BRANCH

Article II of the Constitution sets up the executive branch. This branch is responsible for executing the laws. This means putting laws into effect. The president is elected by US citizens to lead the executive branch.

HEAD OF STATE

The president is the head of state. This means he or she runs the executive branch. This includes running the US military forces. The president also represents the United States to the rest of the world. He or she meets with world leaders. Together, they

The president lives and works at the White House in Washington, DC. All US presidents except George Washington have lived at the White House.

The president meets with other world leaders. In 2022, President Joe Biden met with Ukrainian president Volodymyr Zelensky.

discuss wars and other issues. They talk about trade between countries. The president can make deals with other countries too. These may involve trade or military agreements.

The Constitution says the president must make reports to Congress. The president must give Congress "Information of the State of the Union."[4] Once a year, the president gives a speech to Congress. This is called the State of the Union Address. It usually describes current issues of concern. In the speech, the president often asks Congress to pass laws to address problems.

The president can also issue executive orders. These are different from laws. They affect only how the executive branch works. Most orders are minor. But some have changed history. In 1948, President Harry Truman issued Executive Order 9981. It ended racial **segregation** in the US military.

Executive orders can be challenged in court. Judges can strike down orders that are improper. They can reject orders that go beyond a president's power. This happened to a 2017 order issued by President Donald Trump. The order stated that people from certain countries could not enter the United States. Many people challenged this order. Courts struck it down. They said the order violated federal laws and the Constitution.

President Harry Truman signed an executive order that banned racial segregation in the US military.

Congress can also fight back against executive orders. If Congress opposes an order, it can pass a law to cancel it. Congress may also refuse to give the president money to enforce an order. The president must follow the laws that Congress enacts. Presidents often ask

Congress to pass certain laws. But Congress makes its own decisions.

TOP OFFICIALS

Many people work for the president. One is the vice president, who is elected with the president. He or she steps in as president if the president cannot serve.

Most executive branch officials are not elected. The president chooses people for about 4,000 top positions. About 1,200 of these positions require Senate approval.

The president also chooses advisers to be on his or her cabinet. In 2021, President

The vice president serves as a top adviser to the president. In 2020, Kamala Harris became the first woman to serve as US vice president.

Joe Biden chose twenty-five men and women to be on his cabinet. This includes top officials such as the attorney general, who runs the Department of Justice.

THE EXECUTIVE BRANCH AT WORK

The executive branch is organized into agencies. There are more than 400 of these agencies. Different agencies manage different issues. For example, one agency deals with agriculture. Others handle health, housing, and transportation. Leaders of these agencies report to the president.

More than 4 million people work in the executive branch. Most of these workers are not hired directly by the president. They can

The US Department of the Treasury is one of the executive agencies. These are headquartered in Washington, DC.

stay in their jobs no matter who is president. These workers keep the government running. US Postal Service workers deliver mail. Soldiers defend American interests. Other federal workers include park rangers, lawyers, and scientists.

THE PRESIDENT'S POWER

The country's founders did not want a king. So they limited the president's power. They gave the president a four-year term. This means he or she stays in office for four years. Then there is another presidential election. The president may run

STATE EXECUTIVE BRANCHES

Most state governments have divided executive branches. Voters elect various state officials directly. In one election, they might elect officials from different political parties. This means a governor may have different political views from other officials in the executive branch. But the officials must still work together to run the state government.

for reelection. But voters decide who the next president will be.

In 1787, the Constitution did not say how many terms a president could serve. George Washington was the first president. He stepped down after two terms. Since then, only President Franklin Roosevelt has served more than two terms. He was first elected in 1932. He won his fourth term in 1944. After that, Congress limited the president to two terms.

In times of crisis, people expect the president to act. Sometimes presidents take on greater powers during these times.

Franklin Roosevelt served as president during World War II. He expanded the president's powers to help support the war effort.

During World War II (1939–1945), President Roosevelt expanded the executive power. He said this was needed to run the war effort. This happened again after the **terrorist** attacks of September 11, 2001.

Congress gave the president greater power to catch terrorists.

The United States has changed since the Constitution was written. It is no longer a tiny, new nation. It is a world power. In 1790, the US population was less than 4 million people. In 2022, the population was more than 300 million. The executive branch protects retirement and health benefits. It collects taxes and regulates businesses. It runs an enormous military. It has expanded into areas the country's founders may never have imagined. The president oversees all this.

3

THE JUDICIAL BRANCH

Article III of the Constitution deals with the judicial branch. It sets up the US Supreme Court. Courts and judges decide what the laws mean. They also hold trials of people accused of crimes. And they resolve disputes when one person **sues** another.

THE US COURTS

The country's founders did not want judges to worry about making unpopular decisions. So they decided that federal judges would be appointed. This means federal

The US Supreme Court hears cases at the Supreme Court building in Washington, DC.

In 2022, President Joe Biden nominated Ketanji Brown Jackson as Supreme Court justice. She is the first Black woman to serve on the Supreme Court.

judges do not run for election. Instead, the president nominates them. Judges must then be confirmed by the Senate. Once confirmed, a person can be a judge for life.

The Constitution says judges "shall hold their Offices during good Behavior."[5]

The Constitution also said that Congress could set up the rest of the court system. So Congress passed the Judiciary Act of 1789. This created two levels of courts below the Supreme Court.

THREE LEVELS OF COURTS

The first level is the district courts. There are ninety-four US district courts. Each state has at least one. These courts hold trials. People accused of federal crimes go on trial in district courts. **Civil** trials also happen in these courts. In a civil case, someone asks a court to right a wrong. For example, a worker might argue that she was illegally fired.

During a trial, both sides tell their side of the story. They offer evidence. They may call witnesses to speak. A jury hears this evidence. The jury is a group made up of

STATE COURTS

Each state runs its own courts. In many states, voters elect judges. Unpopular judges can be voted out. State courts hear cases involving state laws. They rule on state crimes, divorces, and family matters. They also hear contract and personal injury cases.

ordinary people. They decide who is telling the truth. The jury listens to the facts of the case. They decide who is guilty or not guilty. Then the judge issues the court sentence based on the facts and the law.

After the trial court decides a case, the losing side can go to a higher court. This is the appeals court. The appeals court reviews the trial court's decision. A panel of three judges hears the appeal. These judges are called justices.

The US courts of appeals are divided into circuits. They are split up by geography. The Ninth Circuit is the largest. It hears appeals

Some judges preside over civil and criminal trials. They keep order in the court, listen to the facts of a case, and decide on court sentences.

from eleven western states and territories, from Guam to California. This circuit has twenty-nine judges.

The courts of appeals do not have juries. They do not decide the facts of a case. Instead, they focus on whether the trial judge made a mistake about the law. If the trial judge was wrong, the appeals court can reverse the decision. Or it can tell the trial judge to fix the mistake.

The highest court is the Supreme Court. It reviews court of appeals decisions. But it does not review them all. The Supreme Court decides which cases to hear. Every year, thousands of people ask the Supreme Court to hear their cases. The court takes about one hundred cases each year. It tries to take only the most important cases.

The Supreme Court has the last word on the meaning of the US Constitution and laws. It can settle disputes between states. Sometimes two courts of appeals disagree about a law. In this situation, the Supreme Court decides which court is correct.

CHECKS ON THE COURTS

The courts are shaped by the other branches. The president nominates judges. But the Senate must review and confirm these nominations. Congress also passes laws affecting the courts. It decides how much money the courts get. It sets the number of judges too. In 1869, Congress

In 2023, there were nine Supreme Court justices. John Roberts (center front) served as chief justice, while the others were associate justices.

decided the court would have a chief justice and eight associate justices.

Congress can impeach judges too. Federal judges are appointed for life. But Congress can remove a judge if he or she commits a serious crime.

4
BALANCING THE BRANCHES

The country's founders wanted the people to hold power over the government. They designed the government in a way that made this possible. The US system of checks and balances may not work perfectly. But it still stands.

TITLE IX

Each branch of government pushes against the other two. No one branch gets everything it wants. But together, the three branches shape the nation's laws.

Scales are sometimes used as a symbol of checks and balances. They represent how each branch balances out the other two.

A good example is Title IX (Title Nine). This law was passed in 1972. It requires schools to provide equal treatment regardless of gender. It applies to schools that receive federal money.

The Department of Education is in the executive branch. It enforces Title IX. It tells schools how to follow the law.

FEDERALISM

Besides creating three branches, the Constitution limits government power in another way. It splits power between the national and state governments. This is called federalism. State governments control state courts, businesses, schools, and other local issues. But when state laws conflict with federal laws, federal laws have control.

In 1983, a Title IX case went to the Supreme Court. It involved a school that did not directly receive federal money. But its students got financial aid. The court said Title IX applied only to the program receiving federal money, not the whole school.

Congress disagreed. In 1988, it passed a new bill. This bill covered schools whose students received federal aid. It said Title IX applied to all those schools' programs. President Ronald Reagan vetoed the bill. But Congress overrode the veto.

Congress passing a law is not always the end of the story. In 2022, the Department of Education proposed changes to Title IX. These would increase protections for students, including LGBTQ students.

CONGRESS INVESTIGATES

Congress can also investigate the other branches. The Constitution does not mention this power. But the courts decided that it is part of the lawmaking power. Many people believe Congress's investigations protect democracy. Woodrow Wilson was the twenty-eighth US president. He said Congress "is meant to be the eyes and the voice" of voters.[6]

Congress's investigation of the Watergate scandal led to President Richard Nixon's resignation.

In the 1970s, for example, Congress investigated the Watergate scandal. This involved illegal activities by President Richard Nixon's reelection committee. Congress found out that Nixon was involved. Because of this, Nixon resigned from the presidency.

On January 6, 2021, supporters of former president Trump attacked the US Capitol. Joe Biden had won the presidential election. Trump's supporters said the election was rigged. Congress investigated this. It found that Trump was responsible for the attack. It recommended criminal charges against him. But Congress cannot charge someone with a crime. The Department of Justice, in the executive branch, has that task. In 2022 and 2023, it continued investigating Trump's role in the attack in order to make a decision about any possible charges. If the Department of Justice brings charges

A House committee investigated the January 6, 2021, attack on the US Capitol.

against someone, the case will go before the courts within the judicial branch.

The split of powers among the branches can sometimes cause delays. But it makes the US government work. By working together, the branches serve the people.

GLOSSARY

civil

involving citizens and their interests, rights, and concerns

committees

official groups of people in charge of a specific issue, topic, or task

delegates

people serving as representatives at a government meeting

nominates

recommends a person to be considered for a government position

segregation

the separation of people based on their race

sues

brings legal charges against another person

terrorist

a person who uses extreme violence to achieve a certain goal or create fear

treaties

agreements made between two groups or nations

tyranny

unjust or cruel power

SOURCE NOTES

CHAPTER ONE: THE LEGISLATIVE BRANCH

1. "The Constitution of the United States: A Transcription," *National Archives*, February 3, 2023. www.archives.gov.

2. James Madison, "Federalist No. 47: The Particular Structure of the New Government and the Distribution of Power Among Its Different Parts," *Federalist Papers: Primary Documents in American History*, February 1, 1788. www.loc.gov.

3. "The Constitution of the United States: A Transcription."

CHAPTER TWO: THE EXECUTIVE BRANCH

4. "The Constitution of the United States: A Transcription."

CHAPTER THREE: THE JUDICIAL BRANCH

5. "The Constitution of the United States: A Transcription."

CHAPTER FOUR: BALANCING THE BRANCHES

6. Woodrow Wilson, "Congressional Government: Conclusion," *Teaching American History*, 1885. https://teachingamericanhistory.org.

FOR FURTHER RESEARCH

BOOKS

Jill Abramson, *What Is Congress?* New York: Penguin Workshop, 2021.

Janie Havemeyer, *Rule by the People*. San Diego, CA: BrightPoint Press, 2024.

Karen Kellaher, *The Presidency: Why It Matters to You*. New York: Children's Press, 2020.

INTERNET SOURCES

"Branches of the U.S. Government," *USA.gov*, February 9, 2023. www.usa.gov.

"My Congressional District," *United States Census Bureau*, n.d. www.census.gov/mycd.

"Separation of Powers with Checks and Balances," *Bill of Rights Institute*, n.d. https://billofrightsinstitute.org.

WEBSITES

Congress
www.congress.gov

The US Congress website offers current information about members, bills, committees, and other matters related to the business of Congress.

United States Courts
www.uscourts.gov

The United States Courts website provides information about the US court system, its history, and its rules.

The White House
www.whitehouse.gov

The official White House website provides information about the US government and its history.

INDEX

Biden, Joe, 33, 56
bills, 16, 17–21, 53

checks and balances, 10, 22–23, 25, 50
colonists, 10
committees, 16, 18, 20, 55
Congress, 6–8, 9, 12–25, 29, 31–32, 37, 39, 43, 48–49, 53, 54–56
Courts of Appeals, 9, 45–47, 48

district courts, 9, 43–45

elections, 15, 36–37, 42, 55, 56
England, 10
executive branch, 8, 9, 26–39, 52, 56
executive orders, 29–31

federalism, 52

House of Representatives, 9, 13, 15, 16, 17–20, 23

impeachment, 23, 25, 49

January 6, 2021, 56
judges, 30, 40–43, 44, 45–47, 48–49
judicial branch, 8, 9, 40–49, 57
Judiciary Act of 1789, 43
juries, 44–45, 46

legislative branch, 8, 9, 12–25

Madison, James, 22

Nixon, Richard, 55
nominations, 25, 42, 48
nonvoting house members, 16

presidential terms, 36–37
presidents, 6–8, 9, 21–22, 25, 26–35, 36–39, 42, 48, 53, 54–56

Revolutionary War, 10
Roosevelt, Franklin, 37–38

Senate, 9, 13–15, 17–20, 23, 25, 32, 42, 48
State of the Union Address, 29
Supreme Court, 9, 40, 43, 47–48, 53

Title IX, 51–54
trials, 25, 40, 43–45, 46–47
Truman, Harry, 30
Trump, Donald, 30, 56

US Constitution, 8–11, 12, 16–17, 22–23, 26, 29, 30, 37, 39, 40, 43, 47, 52, 54

vetoes, 6, 8, 21–22, 53
vice presidents, 9, 32
voting, 13, 15, 16, 18, 20, 22, 25, 36, 37, 44, 54

Watergate scandal, 55
World War II, 38

IMAGE CREDITS

Cover (left): © lucky-photographer/iStockphoto
Cover (middle): © lucky-photographer/iStockphoto
Cover (right): © Brandon Moser/iStockphoto
5: © Kaspars Grinvalds/Shutterstock Images
7: © Mark Reinstein/Shutterstock Images
9: © Red Line Editorial
11: © doublediamondphoto/iStockphoto
13: © S. Borisov/Shutterstock Images
14: © Craig Hudson/Sipa USA/Alamy
19: © Rob Crandall/Shutterstock Images
21: © Adam Schultz/The White House
24: © Maxim Elramsisy/Shutterstock Images
27: © Luca Perra/Shutterstock Images
28: © Salma Bashir Motiwala/Shutterstock Images
31: © Harris & Ewing/Library of Congress
33: © Lev Radin/Shutterstock Images
35: © Mihai_Andritoiu/Shutterstock Images
38: © OWI/Library of Congress
41: © Steven Frame/Shutterstock Images
42: © White House Photography/Shutterstock Images
46: © gorodenkoff/iStockphoto
49: © Fred Schilling/Collection of the Supreme Court of the United States
51: © zendograph/Shutterstock Images
55: © magnez2/iStockphoto
57: © Lev Radin/Shutterstock Images

ABOUT THE AUTHOR

Christy Mihaly is a former lawyer and author of more than thirty books for young readers. She has worked for the executive branch of the state of Vermont in the attorney general's office. She has also worked for the judicial branch of California at the state supreme court and has testified before state and local legislatures. She has written books about the US government for readers of all ages.